JEROME G BROWN

THE YOUNG INVESTOR'S HANDBOOK

UNDERSTANDING ASSET CLASSES

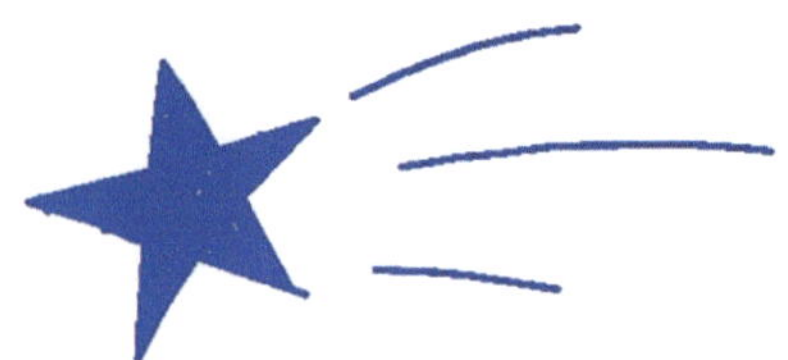

TO ALL THE AMBITIOUS INVESTORS ...

... who are dedicated to building a secure financial future for themselves and their families,

It is with great pleasure and heartfelt dedication that I present this comprehensive A-Z guide on understanding asset classes. As a seasoned investor myself, I recognize the importance of equipping oneself with the necessary knowledge and tools to make informed investment decisions.

This ebook is a culmination of my extensive research, investment experience, and expertise in finance. I have written this guide with a single-minded focus on providing aspiring investors with a detailed understanding of the various asset classes available in the market, their features, and how to evaluate and select them for investment purposes.

As you embark on this journey towards financial freedom, I urge you to make the most of the information presented in this book. By doing so, you will be able to make sound investment decisions, minimize risks, and maximize returns.

Finally, I would like to express my gratitude to all those who supported me in writing this ebook. Special thanks go to my family, friends, and colleagues who provided me with the encouragement and motivation to see this project through.

May this ebook be a valuable asset to you in your investment journey, and may you reap the benefits of sound financial planning and investment choices.

Sincerely,

Jerome G. Bronn

The more you learn, the more you earn
FRANK CLARK

TABLE OF CONTENT

HEY YOUNG INVESTOR!

Thank you for picking up a copy of our guide. We're so glad you're here!

We believe it's never too soon to learn about money, that's why we created this guide to provide young readers like you with an insight into the most important and exciting concepts of finance and investing, teaching you all the basics you need to know about different assets.

As you probably already know, money is an essential part of our lives, and learning how to handle it properly is really important from a young age. By understanding the basics of finances, you can develop good habits that will serve you now and all the way into adulthood.

In this ebook, we will talk about a range of different assets, so that you have a deeper understanding of what each one is, how it works, and how you can buy it. We've also included an A-Z list of asset classes and financial vocabulary so that you can learn how to use some new words on the topic.

Remember, the sooner you know how to handle money, the sooner you'll be able to live comfortably where you can follow your dreams and live the life you wish to live. Investing can bring you the stability you need, especially if you start young, stay dedicated, and continue to educate yourself about the process.

So, are you ready to learn a valuable set of skills and ideas that can transform the way you live your entire life?

Great! We're excited to teach you.

Let's get straight to the exciting stuff.

MONEY

WHAT IS MONEY?

You've most likely known about money for as long as you can remember.

But, what is it exactly?

Money is something that people use to buy and sell things they need or want. You can use different forms of money to pay for things, for example, coins like nickels and dimes, paper bills like one-dollar notes, or digital currencies, like paying with your cell phone (Google or Apple Pay) or with a debit or credit card.

WHY DO PEOPLE NEED MONEY?

People need money for many, many different things. In its simplest form, we use money to take care of our most basic needs like having food to eat and a home to live in. However, money can also help you to achieve your goals, by paying for education or empowering you to start your own business.

When you have more money, or at least enough money, you can live a comfortable life with a high standard of living where you don't need to worry about bills or getting access to things that you need to survive.

HOW CAN WE MAKE MONEY GROW?

When you pay your money to buy a product or service, that money is gone forever to the person or business you gave it to in exchange for what you bought. That's why we need to find ways to make our money grow and duplicate all the time so that we have a continual flow of cash that we can use to pay for things.

Making your money grow is what we'll be talking about all the way through this ebook. We're going to show you the different investment options to help your money start growing really soon so that you never have to worry about running out.

Ready to learn more?
Great! Let's keep going.

STOCKS

WHAT ARE STOCKS?

Company stocks are sold on the stock market. This is a particular marketplace where companies sell shares (ownership percentages of their company) to raise funds for things like business improvements, team growth, inventory or anything else they need to help their business succeed.

Investing in shares is a potentially profitable way to grow your wealth as the value of shares may increase in time, resulting in you gaining a profit when you decide to sell them again. Additionally, owning shares may entitle you to receive a payout at different times. These payouts are called dividends.

HOW DO STOCKS WORK?

Let's take a look at a simple example rather than talking about massive companies right away.

Imagine you start baking cookies at home with the hope of making a little money to buy a video game you really want. You start selling your cookies to your friends and with that, you see that they like them. Since they like them so much, they become a product that they're willing to pay for, and so your new business idea becomes profitable, proving you with money from the cookies you're selling.

Over time, your cookies become so popular that you decide to make more cookies to keep up with the demand. However, to be able to buy the things you need to make the cookies (like flour, butter, and sugar), you need money - money you don't currently have.

So, what do you do?

One option is to sell shares of your cookie business to other people who believe you're going to make a profit. When someone buys a share of your cookie business, they become a part-owner. They've given you money to help you make more cookies, and in return, they will get a share of the profits once you start selling the cookies again.

Stocks work the same way, but instead of your cookie business, it can be a company in any sector. When you buy a share of a company's stock, you become a part-owner of that company.

How do you become a part-owner?

Because you've given the company money to help it grow and make more profits, and in return, you get a share of those profits.

When the company does well, you'll make money as the value of your share you own will go up. That means if you sell it, you'll get more than what you initially paid for it - and, that's the whole concept. By buying shares, you become a part-owner of a company, and you have a chance to make money if the company does well.

Pretty simple, right?

HOW DO YOU BUY STOCKS?

As a small-scale investor, you can buy stocks by paying for them through a brokerage. A brokerage works like a shop for stocks, acting as a middleman between buyers and sellers who want to buy and sell their stocks. Joining a brokerage is kind of like when you sign up for a bank account, however, it connects you to a different financial service.

EXAMPLES OF STOCKS

Some of your favorite, or best-known companies, likely sell stocks on the stock market. Some examples include:

- Disney
- Apple
- Amazon
- Coca-Cola Company
- Nintendo

BONDS

WHAT ARE BONDS?

A bond is a type of investment where you give someone (like a company or the government) some money and they promise to pay you back with extra money, called interest. It's like loaning your friend some money to buy a snack at recess, and they promise to pay you back with extra money (interest) when they can.

HOW DO BONDS WORK?

Bonds are a way for companies or governments to borrow money from people. Generally, they use this money to fund projects or pay for expenses. In return, they promise to pay the bondholder back with interest. Bonds can be a solid investment option as they are considered less risky than investing in stocks; however, they don't tend to be as profitable.

For example, let's say you have $200 and you buy a bond from a company. The company promises to pay you back your $200 plus an extra $10 in a year.

This means you'll get $210 back in total, which means you just made a profit and gained more money than you put in. That's money growth!

HOW DO YOU BUY BONDS?

There are a couple of different ways that people buy bonds. One of the most popular options is through a brokerage, as we already mentioned with stocks. The other is to buy it directly from the company selling them. Some companies or government agencies might offer bond purchase options on their websites or through their bond departments, this just cuts out the role of the brokerage that generally connects buyers with sellers, and vice versa.

EXAMPLES OF BONDS

- **US Treasury Bonds** - Issued by the government to fund operations.

- **Corporate Bonds** - Issued by companies to raise money for different purposes.

- **Municipal Bonds** - Issued by state and local governments to raise money for public projects, like schools.

- **High-Yield Bonds** - These are bonds that offer higher interest rates but come with higher risks due to the lower credit ratings of the issuers.

- **Zero-Coupon Bonds** - These are bonds that don't pay regular interest but are sold at a discount to their face value and pay the full face value at maturity.

REAL ESTATE

WHAT IS REAL ESTATE?

Real estate is another word for land or buildings that people buy.

HOW DOES REAL ESTATE WORK?

People buy real estate for various reasons. Some buy it to live in it themselves, while others buy it to rent it out to other people. It can also be bought and sold for investment purposes, which means people buy it in the hope that its value will increase over time, allowing them to sell it for a profit.

When someone owns real estate, it means they have the right to use and control that property as they wish. For example, if someone owns a house, they can live in it, rent it out to someone else, or sell it to someone who wants to live in it or rent it out. This gives you plenty of options - especially as an investor.

HOW DO YOU BUY REAL ESTATE?

You can work with a realtor, who specializes in selling real estate, or you can buy it directly from the previous owner of the property.

EXAMPLES OF REAL ESTATE

- Houses
- Apartments
- Stores
- Warehouses
- Land without a building on it

COMMODITIES

WHAT ARE COMMODITIES?

In simple terms, the word commodities refer to things that people use every day. For example, food, clothing, and fuel. They are things that can be bought and sold, just like a candy bar or a video games.

However, unlike candy bars or video games, commodities are things that are naturally produced by nature, like crops that are grown on farms, or minerals that are mined from the ground.

They are often raw materials that are used to make other things, which makes them hugely valuable.

HOW DO YOU BUY COMMODITIES?

Commodities are bought and sold on exchanges and through brokerages, just like stocks and bonds. In the same way, you buy stocks and bonds, investors buy commodities in the hope that their value will go up over time, allowing them to sell them for a profit.

EXAMPLES OF COMMODITIES

- Coffee
- Gold
- Oil
- Silver
- Copper

MUTUAL FUNDS AND ETFS

WHAT ARE MUTUAL FUNDS AND ETFS?

Instead of picking individual stocks, you can buy a mutual fund or an ETF, which is a group of stocks that are managed by a professional fund manager. With a mutual fund, you buy shares in the fund and the fund manager uses that money to buy a variety of different stocks. The goal is to build a diversified portfolio that can potentially earn higher returns than if you invested in just one or a few stocks on your own.

An ETF works similarly but is traded on a stock exchange like a stock. It also tracks a specific "index" or group of stocks.

HOW DO THEY WORK?

When you invest in a mutual fund or ETF, you own a small piece of each of the stocks in the fund. This helps spread out your risk rather than investing all of your money into one stock. If one of the stocks in the fund goes down, the others may still do well, which helps to balance out your losses, and increase your potential for steady wins.

HOW DO YOU BUY MUTUAL FUNDS AND ETFS?

Through a brokerage - just like stocks, commodities and bonds.

EXAMPLES OF MUTUAL FUNDS AND ETFS

- Vanguard Total Stock Market Index Fund
- SPDR S&P 500 ETF Trust
- Fidelity Contrafund
- PowerShares QQQ

ALTERNATIVE INVESTMENTS

WHAT ARE ALTERNATIVE INVESTMENTS?

Alternative investments are investments that are different from traditional investments like stocks, bonds, and real estate. They are called "alternatives" because they are not as commonly known or used, but they can still be profitable.

People use alternative investments to diversify their investment portfolios and potentially earn higher returns. They may also invest in them because they include items that generally interest them.

EXAMPLES OF ALTERNATIVE INVESTMENTS

- Art
- Collectibles like sneakers, watches, coins, stamps
- Cryptocurrency
- Precious metals

SAVING VS. INVESTING

WHAT DOES IT MEAN TO SAVE?

Saving money means putting aside some of our money for a future goal. This could be for a toy we want to buy, a trip we want to take, or for something bigger like college or a car. When we save our money, we are putting it in a safe place so we can use it when we need it.

WHAT IS INVESTING

Investing is when we use our money to buy things that we hope will grow in value over time. This could be buying shares of a company, buying a bond, or investing in real estate. Investing can help our money grow faster than just saving it in a bank account. However, investing also comes with risks, so we need to be careful and do our research before making any investment decisions.

SHORT-TERM AND LONG-TERM GOALS

It's important to think about both short-term and long-term goals when saving and investing. Short-term goals are things we want to do or buy in the near future, like buying a new bike or going to a concert. Long-term goals are things we want to do or buy in the future but may take many years to save for, like going to college or buying a house.

THE BENEFITS OF INVESTING

When we invest our money, it can grow faster than if we just save it in a bank account. Over time, our money can earn interest or grow in value, which means we could have more money in the future than we started with. Investing can also help us achieve our long-term goals, like buying a house or saving for retirement. In this chapter, we learned that saving and investing are important for achieving our financial goals.

By saving our money, we can prepare for the things we want to do or buy in the future, while investing can help us grow our money over time. Remember, it's important to have both short-term and long-term goals and to do our research before making any investment decisions.

INFLATION

In this chapter, we will learn about inflation and how investing in certain asset classes can help us stay ahead of it.

WHAT IS INFLATION

Have you ever noticed that the price of things seems to go up over time? This is because of inflation. Inflation is when the cost of goods and services increases over time, which means the value of our money decreases.

For example, if a candy bar costs $1 today and inflation is 2% per year, next year that same candy bar might cost $1.02. Staying Ahead of Inflation: So, what can we do to stay ahead of inflation? One way is to invest in certain asset classes.

Some investments, like stocks and real estate, can grow in value over time and can even outpace inflation. This means that if we invest our money wisely, we can potentially earn more money than if we just kept it in a bank account.

CHOOSING THE RIGHT INVESTMENTS

Of course, not all investments are created equal. Some investments are riskier than others and may not be right for everyone. It's important to do our research and talk to a grown-up before making any investment decisions. We should also remember that past performance is not a guarantee of future results, so even if an investment has done well in the past, it may not continue to do so in the future.

In this chapter, we learned that inflation can impact the value of our money over time, but investing in certain asset classes can help us stay ahead of it. By choosing the right investments and doing our research, we can potentially earn more money than if we just kept our money in a bank account.

SOCIALLY RESPONSIBLE INVESTING

In this chapter, we will learn about socially responsible investing and how we can make a positive impact with our investments.

WHAT IS SOCIALLY RESPONSIBLE INVESTING?

Have you ever heard of socially responsible investing? This is when investors consider not only the financial returns of their investments, but also the social and environmental impact. For example, an investor might choose to invest in companies that are working to reduce their carbon footprint, or in companies that are committed to fair labor practices.

MAKING A POSITIVE IMPACT

By investing in socially responsible companies, we can make a positive impact on the world around us. For example, if we invest in companies that are committed to sustainable practices, we can help reduce our carbon footprint and protect the environment. If we invest in companies that treat their employees fairly, we can help promote social justice and equality.

DOING OUR RESEARCH

Of course, it's important to do our research before investing in any company. We should make sure that the companies we invest in are truly committed to social and environmental responsibility, and that they are also financially sound. We should also remember that investing always involves some degree of risk, and that past performance is not a guarantee of future results.

In this chapter, we learned about socially responsible investing and how we can make a positive impact with our investments. By investing in companies that are committed to social and environmental responsibility, we can help create a better world for ourselves and future generations.

IMPORTANT TO KNOW ABOUT ALL INVESTMENTS

No matter what type of investment you're looking into it's important to think about the following topics.

Once you consider these, you will have a higher chance of making better decisions about your investments which will get you the biggest return.

DIVERSIFICATION

It's important to diversify your investments across different asset classes. This helps to reduce risk. By spreading your money across different types of assets, you can help protect your portfolio from losses if one particular asset class performs poorly. As your Grandma used to say "don't put all your eggs in one basket".

RISK VS. RETURN

Different asset classes come with different levels of risk and potential return. Generally, the higher the potential return, the higher the risk. It's important to understand your risk tolerance and invest accordingly.

TIME HORIZON

Your investment time horizon is the length of time you plan to hold your investments. Different asset classes may be more or less suitable depending on your time horizon. For example, stocks may be a good choice for long-term investments, while bonds may be more appropriate for shorter-term goals.

COSTS

It's important to understand the costs associated with investing in different asset classes. Fees and expenses can eat into your returns, so it's important to choose investments with low fees and expenses whenever possible.

THE A TO Z GUIDE OF ASSET CLASSES

Just like you learned your ABCs in the first year of school, it's helpful to know the ABCs of finances.

This will make sure you know all the words that might come up about finance, and understand how you can use them in your own conversations with family and friends.

We have included an example sentence for each word so you can instantly know how to use it yourself when you're ready.

A IS FOR ASSET.

Assets are things that have value and can be owned, such as money, real estate, or investments. Examples of assets include a savings account, a car, ETFs, or a house.

"Owning a rental property can be a great asset for generating an additional income."

A IS FOR ALTERNATIVE INVESTMENTS.

Alternative investments are investments that are not traditional, such as stocks or bonds. Examples of alternative investments include art, real estate, and cryptocurrencies.

"My cousin decided to diversify his investment portfolio by investing in alternative investments like real estate and commodities, in addition to traditional stocks and bonds."

B IS FOR BONDS.

Bonds are a type of investment where you can lend money to a company or government in exchange for interest payouts. They are less risky than stocks, however, don't offer as much money in return. When the bond "matures", the person who lent the money gets their original investment back.

"My grandma gave me a bond for my birthday. I'm going to hold onto it until it matures so that I gain more than she paid for it!"

C IS FOR CASH.

Cash is physical money like coins and bills that you can use to buy things. It's important to learn how to manage your cash wisely, keeping it safe and storing some away for emergencies.

"James wanted to buy a new game at the toy store, but he realized he didn't have enough cash in his wallet, so he decided to save his allowance for a few more weeks."

C IS FOR CRYPTOCURRENCY.

Cryptocurrency is a digital currency that uses cryptography for security. Currencies like Bitcoin, Ethereum, and Dogecoin are decentralized and operate independently of a central bank or government.

"Tom believes that cryptocurrency could be the currency of the future. He already uses it to pay for some things online!"

D IS FOR DERIVATIVES.

Derivatives are financial contracts that gain (or derive) their value from an underlying asset, such as a stock, bond, or commodity.

"Mom purchased a call option on a stock she thought would increase in value. This derivative allowed her to buy the stock at a set price, and she hoped to make a profit if the stock price went up."

E IS FOR EQUITY.

Equity is the value of an asset after you remove any liabilities or debts that are owed on that asset. It can be used in relation to the ownership of a company (stocks or shares) and other assets. For example, when you own a house but are still paying a mortgage on it. In that case, let's say the house is worth $300,000 but you still owe $100,000 on your mortgage. That would mean your equity in the house is $200,000

"Jeff was able to increase his home equity by paying back his mortgage quickly"

F IS FOR FIXED INCOME.

Fixed income is a type of investment that provides a regular, predictable income stream, usually in the form of interest payments. Investors can rely on this fixed income to come in every month, just like a salary.

"My Dad likes to invest in fixed-income securities, like bonds, so that he has a reliable income alongside his job."

G IS FOR GOLD.

Gold is a precious metal that has been used as a form of currency and deemed valuable for thousands of years. It's also a commodity as it can be bought and sold as an investment.

"My Mom got a gold watch for her birthday. She says it will always be valuable as the price of gold always has worth."

H IS FOR HEDGE FUNDS.

Hedge funds are private investment funds that use a variety of strategies to generate returns for their investors. They are generally only available to accredited investors rather than regular investors like you and me.

"Alice's uncle is a wealthy investor who invests his money in hedge funds. They use advanced investment strategies."

I IS FOR INTERNATIONAL INVESTMENTS.

International investments refer to investments made in companies or assets located outside of your home country. For example, if you're living in the US but buy shares in a company in Germany.

"Juan is learning Japanese, so he decided to buy stocks as international investments from Asia"

J IS FOR JUNK BONDS.

Junk bonds are high-yield, high-risk bonds issued by companies with lower credit ratings. Investors who are willing to take on the added risk of investing in junk bonds can potentially earn higher returns, but they also face a greater chance of losing their investment if the issuer defaults on its debt.

"Sandra invested a small amount of money she could afford to lose in a junk bond. I hope it works out for her."

K IS FOR 401(K).

A 401(k) is a retirement savings plan that is sponsored by an employer. Employees can contribute a portion of their pre-tax income to the plan, and the employer may also make matching contributions.

"I'm investing money in my 401(K). Every time I pay a percentage of my income into my retirement fund, my boss pays the same amount! I'm getting double the money"

L IS FOR LENDING.

Lending means providing money to someone else in exchange for interest payments. This can include loans to individuals or businesses and they can be issued privately, through banks or companies that specialize in loans and credits.

"When my uncle Sam needed a new car, he looked into different lending options to find the best interest rate."

M IS FOR MUTUAL FUNDS.

Mutual funds are investment vehicles that pool money from multiple investors to purchase a diversified portfolio of stocks, bonds, or other assets. They are managed by experts who make decisions to try and get the best for everyone. They are thought to be safe investment options.

"Carlos was interested in investing in a diversified portfolio of stocks and bonds. He bought shares in a mutual fund called the Vanguard 500 Index Fund. He was particularly happy that it was run by a professional investment team"

N IS FOR NATURAL RESOURCES.

Natural resources are things that are created in nature, like oil, gas, timber, or minerals, that can be used as important assets for investors.

"Mei believes in sustainability and protecting the environment. That's why she invests her money in renewable natural resource companies that create windmills across the globe"

O IS FOR OPTIONS.

Options are derivatives that give the holder the right, but not the obligation, to buy or sell an underlying asset at a predetermined price.

"Due to my stock options, I can buy more later at a cheaper price"

P IS FOR PRIVATE EQUITY.

Private equity is investments made in private companies that are not traded on public markets (like stocks).

"Juanita and her business partner were able to get funding for their startup idea from a private equity firm. They provided them with the money they needed to grow their business"

Q IS FOR QUALITY.

Quality refers to the characteristics of an asset that make it valuable, such as a company's strong financial history or a property's prime location.

"That company's ability to show strong financial management each year makes them a quality company to invest in."

R IS FOR REAL ESTATE.

Real estate means property such as land, buildings, or homes. It's thought to be a valuable long-term investment as it will always have value.

"I'm planning to invest in real estate as soon as possible. That way I can rent out the space and earn an income"

S IS FOR STOCKS.

Owning a stock means you have part ownership in a company. When you own a stock, you can gain a capital appreciation and dividend income.

"I was given some company stocks as a reward for working with them for 2 years".

T IS FOR TREASURY BILLS.

Treasury bills are short-term debt securities issued by the government. They are sold at a discount to their face value and once they mature, investors will receive the full value of the treasury bill.

"Treasury bills are like IOUs from the government that promise to pay you back the money you loaned them, plus a little extra after a certain amount of time has passed."

U IS FOR UTILITIES.

Utilities refer to companies that provide essential services, such as gas, electricity, or water, to consumers.

"Utilities help people feel comfortable in their home, offering access to essential services like running water and electricity"

V IS FOR VENTURE CAPITAL.

Venture capital is a type of private equity investment that focuses on early-stage startups with high growth potential. Most venture capitalists seek out companies with new and innovative ideas to try and invest and grow their money with the business.

"Stacey was able to start her make-up business as she got funds from a venture capital investor"

W IS FOR WEALTH MANAGEMENT.

Wealth management is a term used when we're talking about managing and investing assets for high-net-worth individuals or families.

"Jeff Bezos has a wealth management team to ensure his money continues to grow"

X IS FOR EXCHANGE-TRADED FUNDS (ETFS).

ETFs are investment funds that are traded on stock exchanges like stocks. They typically track a specific sector and offer investors the ability to gain exposure to a diversified portfolio of assets with a single investment.

"My neighbor wanted to invest in an asset with broad market exposure, so he decided to buy into some ETFs"

Y IS FOR YIELD.

Yield refers to the income generated by an asset, such as interest or dividends.

"That stock is doing really well, so I am able to gain a high yield from my investment"

Z IS FOR ZERO-COUPON BONDS.

These are bonds that don't pay interest but are sold at a discount of their face value. When the bond matures, investors gain full face value.

"In about a year, my zero coupon bond will mature which means I'll get a return on my investment."

THAT'S IT FOR NOW!

Saving and investing in your future can bring you the freedom and stability you need to live the life of your dreams. By starting sooner rather than later, maintaining commitment, investing agressively and continuing your financial education, you could be turning huge profits by the time you hit 30!

We hope this ebook has inspired you to keep learning about investing, assets and how they can give you complete control over your life.

If you're interested in learning more, call or text me on:

 1646 687 4607
Toll free: 1844 430 3984

I'm happy to discuss everything I know with young investors who are ready to enter the world of finance sooner rather than later.

Until next time!

Wealth Creation Family

WealthCreationFamilyCorp.org